Funny Marketing Affected Soft Drink Companies

Funny Marketing Affected Soft Drink Companies

W. Robert Watson

AuthorHouse™ LLC
1663 Liberty Drive
Bloomington, IN 47403
www.authorhouse.com
Phone: 1-800-839-8640

Published by AuthorHouse 02/11/2014

ISBN: 978-1-4817-4182-8 (sc)
ISBN: 978-1-4817-4181-1 (e)

Table of Contents

Foreword

As a preliminary introduction to what I have to share with readers of this story, please understand that the marketing of certain products by a company for which I worked in a sale and marketing capacity has been on my mind for many years.

Though it may appear to do so, the intent of this writing is not intended to poke fun at any of the soft drink companies for some of their botched marketing efforts. Rather, I aim to discuss important variables to successful marketing so that readers of this book can excel in their own efforts and not make mistakes that even great soft drink marketers can make.

Certainly the success of the soft drink company with whom I was previously affiliated had hugely impressive marketing because it was able to take its primary cola product from being developed as a fountain beverage to becoming the most well-known and consumed product in the history of the world. That is cause for marketing awe and not ridicule or humor. Again, there is no intent in this book to be overly critical of this or any other soft drink company. The intent is to show that despite their excellence in marketing, even soft drink companies can make mistakes by not adequately implementing the five Ps of marketing in all of their marketing strategies.

For anyone considering a review of marketing, it never hurts for any companies or individuals who are aware of their own marketing imperfections to know that even companies with the elite reputation and success of certain soft drink companies can still have their less than spectacular marketing moments. All persons involved in the marketing of consumer products need to keep in mind that success is dependent on what is known as the Five Ps of marketing, which are product, package, price, place, and promotion.

Chapter One

History of Some Cola Brands

Looking back many scores of years ago, two of the major soft drink companies charged consumers only a nickel to buy a bottle of their brands. But one of the two major cola companies at that time implemented an advantageous marketing strategy of having a price and package advantage when compared with my company, who was the major competitor. Thus they did a good job with the "P" of promotion by implementing an advertising campaign with a famous commercial that most everyone heard on the radio. In that commercial, it stated that their brand *"hits the spot; twelve full ounces—that's a lot; twice as much for a nickel, too." They concluded the advertisement with the fact that their brand was "the drink for you." In the promotion they were also able to put an emphasis on having both a price and a package advantage.*

Even a student in the most elementary marketing course today should recognize something that the executives of the other soft drink company ignored for twenty-one years following that marketing strategy, and that is the fact that a company marketing decision that allows a competitor to have both a package and price advantage on a similar product will have an adverse effect on the sales and share of market for the company that allows it to happen to them. Thus it was a very positive effect for the soft drink company that had the price and package advantage for a protracted period of time.

It was in the 1930s that they introduced the 12-ounce bottle, selling it for the same nickel price as the 6.5-ounce returnable bottle of their primary competitor. The "twice as much for a nickel too" advertising campaign that ran from 1939 into the 1950s established them as a very effective cola soft drink competitor with a lot of volume and an enhanced share of the market due to a price and package advantage against the primary cola competitor.

Later, other packaging innovations, like the introduction of the sixteen-ounce returnable bottle in 1963, fizzed up the cola wars between the major soft drink manufacturing companies. That was yet another marketing result related to packaging, with companies recognizing that consumers tended to be more prone to accept a sixteen-ounce bottle rather than a twelve-ounce bottle of cola.

In the diet cola realm, the development of a diet cola brand name that used the primary sugar cola brand name but added the word "diet" occurred in 1964, which was a full twenty years before the other major cola company would take what it initially considered to be a "brand name risk" of introducing a beverage with the word "diet" preceding the main brand name. Though that cola company did introduce its first diet cola with a three-letter name a few years after the introduction by the other company, it did so with a formula and taste that was deemed inferior to two of its major cola competitors, resulting in a lower share of the diet market for their brand.

Given what was deemed a little inferior taste, the company tried to improve the market share for the diet cola with a reformulation that improved the taste. The company ran an advertising campaign to promote the improved taste, but it was so close on the heels of the initial introduction of the original diet attempt that, in my opinion, it resulted in most consumers assuming that advertisements for the "new taste" simply meant the taste of the fairly new product, which many consumers had already tried and did not like as well as the other two diet colas.

Thus in spite of marketers having the reputation for marketing prowess and successful introduction of not only their primary brand but having many other successful soft drink products, the company has an amazing history of multiple marketing mistakes that were in addition to giving their primary competitor a price and package advantage for twenty-one years, between 1934 and 1955.

Chapter Two

A New Formula

Again, what one could consider to be the biggest marketing mistake of my company is both in letting its major competitor have a package and price advantage for so many years and, about fifty years later, deciding to reformulate its world-famous brand. That particular decision to reformulate the brand led to the president of their competitor to proudly claim having won the cola wars in a best-selling book he published in 1986. Of course as a side note, the primary purpose seemed to me to be that the author wanted to claim the entire war was in what was happening during the marketing of the primary cola brands of each company—whereas in reality, from what I observed, there were many other marketing battles in which they appeared to have some of their own losses related to marketing.

Ironically, though the reformulation referenced in the 1986 book was viewed as a marketing mistake, a combination of luck and good decisions resulted in a very successful marketing coup that reversed, at least for a period of time, the erosion of the market share for their cola brand in the United States.

But they were not nearly so fortunate in many other soft drink marketing efforts, as can be seen in the stories in this book. All stories are from my own personal experiences beginning in 1969, which was a year well-known in the soft drink world for the "cyclamate crisis," and my marketing involvement ending in 1985 with the introduction of the reformulated brand.

Chapter Three

Other Product Marketing Mistakes

Over that sixteen-year period between 1969 and 1985, I had the good fortune of representing my company in a wide range of marketing capacities, and I was right in the middle of some major marketing thrusts. This marketing involvement included being a district manager for bottler operations based in Salt Lake City for the test market of a green bottle product. A year later I was involved with the company's decision to test market a sports drink in Birmingham. Subsequently, as a senior district manager, I was able to participate in the introduction of a new pepper soda product in the Dallas and Fort Worth area. I was also involved in reviewing the Cola Challenge activities while in Dallas during 1975, and also in 1977 when I was based in Chicago as area marketing manager over ten Midwestern states.

By the early 1980s, I was at the company corporate headquarters and was able to participate in the planning and execution of what was known as the Bottler Structure Project. That project was fascinating, as was the formation of one of its major publicly held bottlers. But is a subject for another book because it related more to financial and business strategies than the marketing strategies and tactics addressed in this book.

Without further dialogue, the following are stories about some marketing mistakes that should be of great interest. The purpose of this marketing review is to provide knowledge and understanding of marketing done by my former company on the way to the market.

Chapter Four

The Cyclamate Crisis

The first story is an intriguing story about soft drink diet beverages that ultimately resulted in good fortune for my employer at the time by achieving an improved market position in comparison to its two major US competitors at the time.

One competitor was the first soft drink company to gain impressive national distribution of a diet cola. The second competitor saw the success of that other competitor and then immediately introduced a brand without using its primary sugar cola name. When it failed to initially achieve the level of marketing success achieved by the first diet cola brand, it then changed the name of the product to include the primary brand name with "diet" in front of it; that achieved better results as it reached number two in the diet cola market, with a slightly smaller share of the market.

My company, which had paid a heavy marketing penalty in its failure to react to market trends in the 1940s and early 1950s, decided to introduce a diet cola, too. But it felt at the time that using the name of the primary brand with a diet beverage would have a potentially adverse effect on the brand name, so it gave the diet cola a unique, three-letter brand name.

I don't know what research on product taste was done prior to the introduction of the brand, but the original formula was not nearly as well received by the public as the other two diet colas on the market. Following the introduction of the diet cola, the product was a distant third in market share.

The company thus made the decision fairly quickly to reformulate the product and develop advertisements and point of sale materials urging consumers to "try the new taste." But as a side marketing point, the decision to spend a lot of money advertising and marketing the product actually resulted in the company having a lot less advertising exposure for their primary name than its major cola competitor, who was able to achieve it by having both the sugar cola and diet cola being advertised with the main brand name.

After reformulating the brand, the change in the formula for the product compared with its initial taste did result in the product tasting significantly better. But the problem was that the company had made a bad first impression with the diet cola product. In spite of a reformulation, it seemed that many consumers assumed that the new product was still the same diet soda as before, and the "new taste" advertisements were simply a reemphasis of that old product. There was little the company did to urge consumers to know that there was a change in the original taste of the brand or to encourage consumers to give it a second try.

While the company languished in the unacceptable position of having the brand as a tertiary diet cola product in the market, fate intervened on behalf of the company with the sudden ban of cyclamates as a sweetener for diet products in the United States. In what seemed to me to be a classic governmental mishandling of a situation, cyclamate was banned based on questionable research and without any forewarning to companies using the product.

The primary alternative non-calorie sweetener was saccharin, which carried a not so good after taste, particularly when compared to cyclamates.

All three companies were certain that the taste of a diet cola sweetened only by saccharin would taste too bad to be accepted by consumers. Each company decided to reformulate the diet cola brands by using a combination of half sugar and half saccharin. The result was a generally acceptable taste with fewer calories than sugar-based colas. But each product still had a lot of calories (seventy-two per can) when compared with the former products using cyclamate and having less than one calorie per serving.

There was one product that my company decided to keep as a true "one calorie or less" product. That product was a diet grapefruit-flavored beverage. Probably the most interesting thing about that decision was that this product had been on the decline after taking the market by storm with its award-winning television advertising campaign. The theme in the TV commercials when the product was originally introduced was to come inside where there was a snow storm going on. The product was advertised as a frosty sugar-free drink. Though it had virtually no calories, indications to me were that a lot of consumers drinking the brand when it was initially introduced were doing so for the unique taste of this grapefruit-based soft drink.

Many of the consumers did not seem to be consuming the beverage because of its low caloric content. The fact that the company decided to focus on the low-calorie feature of the brand after the cyclamate crisis—rather than to launch it as a citrus-based sugar drink—was interesting. It did result in one thing that surprised me and other soft drink marketers. The product gained the highest share of the market of all diet beverages, in spite of it using only saccharin as a sweetener and its inability to have it taste quite as well as it did when using cyclamate.

Given the marketing success of the brand in spite of its less desirable taste, the company realized that many people who were concerned about their diet cared more about caloric content than taste. Therefore the company made the decision to reformulate its diet cola again to be sugar free by taking out the sugar and having it sweetened only with saccharin. The strategy worked extremely well by increasing both the volume and the share of market for the brand. Following that change in product, the brand leaped from its poor number three share of market among the major diet colas to become the number one diet cola, a position it held for over ten years.

The funny thing about the success of this diet cola was not so much that the company lucked out with the cyclamate crisis, but that both major cola competitors refused to follow suit with their diet cola brands for a protracted period of time by reformulating to achieve fewer calories. In spite of (1) seeing the same share of market dominance of the diet grapefruit brand as a sugar-free beverage with dubious virtues for taste, (2) seeing their major competitor's diet cola sales soar immediately after being reformulated without the use of any sugar, and (3) enabling their diet cola competitor to run television commercials showing that one could drink seventy-two glasses of the brand before getting as many calories as one glass of the other two diet colas, both soft drink competitors failed to reformulate and eliminate the marketing advantage. This failure to eliminate the sugar from their diet colas lasted for almost two years. So though the CEO's book referenced earlier may have claimed to have won the cola war, he certainly lost the diet cola war through that marketing mistake.

Chapter Five
Another Green Bottle Drink

Sometimes my soft drink company had what appeared to be the right product at the wrong time or with the wrong marketing strategy. A green bottle product was a classic example of this. If marketed properly, the green bottle drink may have somewhat diminished the awesome success of one of the more successful green bottle products of a major competitor. However perhaps it would not have had too much of an effect on that brand because this new product was a caffeine-free drink, whereas apparently an appealing characteristic of the competitive green bottle drink was its high caffeine content.

But regardless, research by the company had come to the realization and conclusion that no traditional soft drink was being marketed as a pure thirst quencher. There was one primary sports beverage being sold as a thirst quencher, but it was not deemed to be a soft drink in the sense of the word being used by the industry at that time. Therefore my company, having determined that there was a void in the market for a thirst quencher among soft drinks, decided to introduce such a product. The research had also indicated that such a drink should be designed and formulated to appeal to blue-collar workers who worked out in the heat of the day and thus would like to have a cold and thirst-quenching beverage.

The company developed that new soft drink brand, which was an excellent tasting green bottle drink. A lot of research had gone into both the product taste as well as the graphics, which included a lion head on the bottle and on the packaging, which was gold and green. Television advertisements were filmed depicting jungle scenes in which safari hunters reached for this thirst quenching beverage. These television advertisements, as well as the graphics for the packaging, won many awards for their originality and effectiveness.

With a good tasting product, a good advertising campaign, and an identified niche as a thirst quencher, the logical question is, "Why was this product, with the marketing prowess of this soft drink company and the excellent bottler distribution system, not a resounding success?" Well, a funny thing happened on the way to the market. It occurred as a result of the chosen test markets (Salt Lake City and Los Angeles) and the advertising slogan itself. Both Salt Lake City and Los Angeles were deemed to be good markets for the test, because both were markets where there was large consumption of green bottle drinks. Salt Lake City was deemed to be a particularly good test market for multiple reasons. Not only was it a large green bottle soft drink market, but the demographics were heavily skewed toward the middle income, white male, and blue collar workers. Salt Lake City also had a well-balanced media market to run commercials promoting the new product. If any market in the United States should have been a success for a great-tasting, green bottle thirst-quencher soft drink product, it should have been Salt Lake City. The independent bottler in that market was a very well-run operation with a significant market share leadership position against its two largest soft drink competitors.

But the product was never launched in Salt Lake and did very poorly in the Los Angeles test market because of a bad marketing decision related to the advertising slogan, which stated it was "The drink that quenches the African thirst."

Of course the campaign used that term to imply that men shown in the television advertisements, while being on a safari in the heat of Africa, were consuming the beverage to quench their thirst in that country. But the printed advertisement, point of sale material, and billboards simply said that it was a drink to quench the African thirst—which to most people meant the thirst of an African.

Thus the reason for not having a successful test in Salt Lake City was because it was felt that a blue-collar, white construction worker in 1970 would not want to be viewed as a person consuming a drink advertised as being for Africans.

Chapter Six

A Sports Drink

Another good product developed by my company that failed to succeed was one to compete with a sports drink that had been growing at a very successful rate. The product's success caused many soft drink bottlers to question the company about how they planned to counteract the growth of the sports drink.

My company decided to develop a new product and bring all of the tangible and intangible factors necessary to do so. The first step was the product name, and they chose a very good one by using one related to Olympic sports, which made for a highly recognizable trademark. They also notified the Olympic Committee that they would pay a royalty for every unit of their new brand that was sold.

Second, they recognized that they needed to have great advertising to promote the product, and they did so by using athletes and encouraging consumers to support the Olympics with their purchase of the brand. At this point, the company had very effectively done four of the five Ps required for marketing success: product, package, promotion, and price.

From a product perspective, they learned in research that although the competitive sports drink was very popular, people preferred an orange-based drink to the lemon-based drink, which was the only formulation of the competition at the time. Our company decided to make its sports drink as an orange-based drink to have a point of difference and taste preference.

The last step after developing excellent packaging and commercials was to have a test market for this product. But once again a marketing mistake happened on the way to market, and this time it was related to place.

The two major test markets chosen were Denver and Birmingham. The decision to run the test in Birmingham was definitely done to appease the owner of the bottling operation in Birmingham, who had long expressed his displeasure with not having a sports drink to market. The problem was that the choice of Birmingham as a test market could not have been worse. This was the marketing error of choosing the wrong place. One primary reason it was the wrong place was because it was the wrong package. The reason for the latter was because the Birmingham market itself was only about 10 percent cans (with a large percent of the market in returnable bottles and the balance in no-deposit, no-return bottles). With the sports drink product being made available only in cans, this was a marketing problem for a test market in Birmingham. Due to the mistake in place, there was also a marketing issue related to product because the Birmingham market was dominated by colas. Flavors had a very small share of market; in fact, the orange category represented less than 5 percent of the market in Birmingham at the time.

The result was that trying to test the viability of a product when it was seeking to garner share within a package and product segment that represented a very tiny share of the market was like trying to pick up silver with chopsticks. In other words, it was virtually impossible. The result was a test market failure despite having a good tasting product with good advertisements.

What about Denver? I don't know much about that test market, but I can say that they chose an operation in which one of the strongest soft drink cola competitors in the country was the competitor. It was thus not the best place to do a market test. The soft drink competitor in Denver had a dominant two to one market share lead at the time. Our local bottler there had enough problems trying to get market share for its established brands, much less trying to introduce a new sports drink.

Chapter Seven

Non-Cola Success in Texas

I was told by some marketing people that in 1960, my company noted that there was strong growth of non-cola products considered to be pepper soda products. I was told that was a bit of a surprise to company executives, who had always simply considered that flavors of drinks in the pepper soda category had only limited geographical appeal within its home state of Texas. It was decided to introduce a competitive product in Texas. The company tried two different products, yet both failed in test market due to less than exceptional marketing efforts.

However, because of the continued growth of products within the pepper soda category nationally—and the fact that many of their own licensed bottlers around the country were beginning to market those products— the company decided to test market a pepper-flavored product in Waco and in the large markets of Dallas and Fort Worth, plus Houston.

After we developed a product that tasted very similar to the leading pepper-flavored brand, an advertising campaign was launched that asked people to try the product, which was stated to have a smooth and easy taste that "goes down good." To ensure market acceptance, the product was sold to grocery stores at a fraction of normal wholesale prices, resulting in a dramatic share of the market based on Audit and Survey, which measures market share based on sales to stores.

However, even though we were selling during the promotional period, the Nielsen share of market for the new pepper soda product was still dramatically lower than that of the major competitive product. The reason for that was because Nielsen measured sales to consumers and not to the stores. Consumers basically indicated that they preferred the primary pepper soda taste of the number one brand because it was more refreshing and had better carbonation. The marketing decision related to promotion by saying "smooth, easy taste" was obviously not appealing. In fact, I was told that the president of the number one pepper soda stated that the new product that was introduced had just stimulated the taste for his company's product. He went on to state that they had found that whenever the company quit giving away their test product in big promotions, the share of the market dropped down. And that was true.

The marketing mistake on the introduction of the pepper soda was both in product and in promotion as it relates to advertising, because most people did not want a "smooth, easy taste" but rather a more highly carbonated and refreshing taste.

Chapter Eight

An Advertising Surprise Campaign

One of the biggest concerns of our soft drink company during the 1970s related to the marketing campaign by the major cola competitor, which was considered a "challenge campaign." In that campaign, commercials were being run showing consumers taking a blind taste test and choosing their cola over ours. Though our company tried to point out that this was done by the competitor using the initials of M versus Q—in which their cola was always the M and the other was always the Q, and people liked the letter M more than the letter Q—they also knew that the probable reason for the other cola prevailing in these blind taste tests related to the fact that the initial sip of each beverage resulted in a slightly less harsh impact on the tongue for their cola compared with ours. If someone were to take several swallows of each beverage, they felt that our cola would likely do as well if not better than their cola. But it was believed that the sweeter initial taste of their cola was what caused it to win the blind taste test, in the opinion of our advertising and marketing executives.

However, our executives also did not want to run any commercials for their primary cola brand that made mention of the competitor, because they felt that doing so would "honor" the competition. The marketing executives spent a lot of time trying to decide how to run ads that would counter the cola challenge without having both cola brands in the commercial.

That led to the promotional decision to run what was considered to be a surprise campaign using the diet grapefruit brand in comparison with the other company's cola. With this campaign, we took the grapefruit-based diet drink and asked people who said they enjoyed the other cola to taste both brands and comment on which one they liked best.

Some of the people said that they like the diet grapefruit brand the best, and so the company redirected all of its planned media for its major cola brand to run thirty-second commercials featuring people choosing the diet grapefruit brand over the competitive cola as a better tasting drink.

The logic behind that marketing decision was that our company felt that when people saw the commercial, they would decide that taste challenge commercials were ridiculous and invalid, because no one would believe that a diet grapefruit beverage would be preferred over a sugar cola beverage. The diet grapefruit surprise campaign was meant to discredit the cola challenge advertising campaign.

The result, however, was that it did nothing to change the effect of the cola challenge campaign. It did cause the diet grapefruit brand sales to soar to a record high as a result of that dramatic national television advertising campaign, in which the company decided to convert all of its planned ads for the major cola brand to do the challenge campaign using the diet grapefruit brand.

To me, it was obvious that people believing in and curious about the fact that drinkers of the other cola product in the commercial had chosen the diet grapefruit product resulted in the diet grapefruit brand achieving substantial sales and share improvement by the highly added "P" of promotion, because it was a good product marketed nationally (places) at competitive pricing and in good packaging.

Chapter Nine

New Cola Formula

When we realized that our competitor did seem to have a taste preference over the product in these blind taste tests and was still using the challenge campaign as a marketing tool, we decided to reformulate the cola taste so that it would win taste tests versus the primary cola competitor. And most everyone knows what happened. After the public virtually revolted against the change of the original formula for the cola, my company changed the name of the new formula to put "New" in front of the brand name. They brought back the original formula by adding the word "Classic" after the brand name.

One of their major bottlers in Chicago stated what most other bottlers probably felt when he said, "Having 'new' in front of the brand name on the package is like having HIV/AIDS on it."

As for the cola war, the series of battles between these two companies became so intense during the 1980s that it turned what I viewed as the senior officers of each company into celebrities. Following the reformulation of the major cola brand, our company president said in an interview, "There is a twist to this story which will please every humanist and will probably keep Harvard professors puzzled for years."

He went on to state, "The simple fact is that all the time and money and skill poured into consumer research on the new formula could not measure or reveal the deep and abiding emotional attachment to original formula felt by so many people." The company president went on to answer any speculation about the reformulation of the brand by stating, "We're not that dumb, and we're not that smart."

Prior to the "less than dumb" and "less than smart" actions of the company related to the reformulation of its world-famous cola brand, there were some other pretty amazing marketing faux pas.

Summary and Conclusion

After a major marketing success for about fifty years, the company made its biggest marketing mistake by letting its primary cola competitor have both a price and package advantage with "twice as much for a nickel, too." But following that marketing mistake, there were none other for the primary brand until the attempt to reformulate the brand, which actually turned out to be somewhat of a marketing benefit because it generated intense consumer loyalty and commitment to the brand.

However, there were many other marketing blunders, and it goes to show that the five Ps of marketing must always be considered and well implemented to ensure success of the sale of consumer products.

In the examples I gave, with the initial introduction and subsequent success of their first diet cola product, it was primarily the "P" of product (i.e., taste) that caused it to not do well initially in sales and share. Then there was the product "virtue" of no calories versus its competitors, which caused it to go from number three in share of the diet market to the number one.

As for the green bottle beverage referenced earlier, in spite of having a great product and packaging and good places to test, the poor promotional slogan killed the product. The "P" of place was the demise of the sports drink, which likewise had a great product, package, promotion, and price.

The pepper soda actually had most of the Ps done well; the Texas markets were a good place for the beverage, the product and packaging were good, and the price was very competitive. The only possible negative was the decision to use "smooth, easy taste"—the promotion of the brand—which was not well received.

Lastly, the new cola formula only had one major negative P, and that was promotion by advertising the change of the brand formula. The new taste had been chosen in blind taste tests as preferred over both the existing cola and competitive cola brands, and so there is the distinct possibility that had the company opted to make an unannounced formula change—and perhaps even used the advertising challenge approach of them "winning" over all colas in blind taste tests—it may have worked.

The five Ps of marketing need to be seriously considered and well implemented to ensure success for any consumer product. Otherwise, some funny things can happen on the way to market.

About the Author

The author served in the soft drink industry as a company district manager based in Salt Lake City and subsequently as a district manager in Birmingham, Alabama. He then was a senior district manager in Dallas and a regional manger in New Orleans and New York. He also served as a Chicago-based area marketing manager for over ten Midwestern states.

By the early 1980s, he was at the corporate headquarters and was able to participate in the planning and execution of what was known as the Bottler Structure Project. That project, which was subsequently followed by the formation of a publicly held company of his corporation, was fascinating, as was the formation of the publicly held company, which has subsequently been acquired by the corporation.

About the Book

The stories in this book include a lot of marketing decisions, some of which include marketing mistakes that should be of great interest. The purpose of this marketing review is to provide knowledge of the marketing implemented by a major soft drink company on the way to the market, and to ensure that readers have a full understanding of the importance of what are known as the five Ps of marketing.